W0114094

DEBT RITUAL

DEBT RITUAL

KATIE NAUGHTON

BUNNY

BUNNY, an imprint of Fonograf Editions
Portland, OR

Copyright © 2025 by Katie Naughton • All rights reserved
Cover and text design by Mike Corrao

First Edition, First Printing

BUNNY07

Published by BUNNY c/o Fonograf Editions
www.bunnypresse.org
www.fonografeditions.com

For information about permission to reuse any
material from this book, please contact BUNNY at
bunnypresse@gmail.com.

ISBN: 978-1-964499-30-7
ISBN (ebook): 978-1-964499-31-4

[clmp]

Fonograf Editions is a proud member of the Community
of Literary Magazines and Presses

CONTENTS

THRESHOLD / 1

DEBT RITUAL: OYSTERS / 2

DEBT RITUAL: SNACK / 3

DEBT RITUAL: GRAIN / 4

DEBT RITUAL: ORGINARY OBJECTS / 6

DEBT RITUAL: MALL / 7

DEBT RITUAL: VALUE / 9

DEBT RITUAL: MASS / 11

DEBT RITUAL: CLASS / 12

DEBT RITUAL: NANTUCKET / 13

DEBT RITUAL: CONGEAL / 14

DEBT RITUAL: DRIFT / 16

DEBT RITUAL: MATERIAL / 17

DEBT RITUAL: MIDDLE / 18

DEBT RITUAL: MUSKRAT LODGE / 20

DEBT RITUAL: SAVINGS BANK / 21

DEBT RITUAL: BUS / 23

DEBT RITUAL: UTOPIA / 24

THRESHOLD

a word is a theory
of how things separate
in threshold wheat
trampled to grain
and chaff and
where this work
happens in a building
or adjacent to it
it's a hard desire
to be only one thing
to sink into time
and know you belong
so erect words
and rituals the
proper scent
of soap the place
for the best
cured meats
cheeses bread
the lists of money
and restaurants
the pleasure song
of consumption
would like
to know it's
best would like
the walls
to be made
of mouths
but buildings
are theories
of how
things separate

DEBT RITUAL: OYSTERS

buy the oysters anyway
each night you spend
in the city and not home
in an apartment alone
costs upwards of fifty dollars
and for what it's worth
oysters are mostly labor
a man at a counter
crushed ice this skill
not out of place in a Whitman
poem what you want
in an oyster is immediacy
brine of a small ocean
and the time to occupy
the texture and material
of this one moment of your
life the brightness in the dark
red leather banquettes gin
and lemon silk suede
and weather the refractions
in the water it isn't right exactly
to want what money has

DEBT RITUAL: SNACK

a tiny perfect pie
in a sealed plastic tin
what I cannot
afford in fashion
I buy novelty
in snacks: life
of the street
buying
food a place
to sit if
not the greater
pleasures

DEBT RITUAL: GRAIN

*(with debt owed to Roland Barthes
"The Grain of the Voice")*

I never wanted money anyway I wanted
texture
which money seems to have
its own texture
not the texture everything else has
like you can pay for thought-
fulness that smooths
what you want to be smooth and
make particular what you want
to pay for
to make money life-
like but like life that's money-
like
singled out and beautiful
which makes art
a problem
confused with money
me too
it seems having
sought
a textural pleasure
written into wanting
patterns of light and shadow
on the faces of people
from some other
time or place put
to film or
imagination or memory
coming out of a dark room
onto the street in the middle of a work day

in an expensive city
and believing
a way to feel this
the grain in money
as a grain in money
my voice my hand
the lemon the leather the light
I bought I wrote
to place myself
to make a name

DEBT RITUAL: ORGINARY OBJECTS

Running in the cold the ritual
of what remains essential:
the body and its care the
necessary conditions of making
sound my footfalls and hard
breath-vector cars of course
when it's cold like this sound
travels differently and scent
it's quiet and more pronounced
the sound the smell the city makes
meat searing and the particularly
upwardly mobile lower middle class
1990s scent of one kind of laundry
detergent an expensive version
at a regular supermarket. I'm thinking
about originary objects the already-
retro orange madras beach towel
I thought would always be what
a beach towel was the weave
of silence and echo the steep valley
made of the lake in June

DEBT RITUAL: MALL

this is about beauty
being a teenager in the mall
like America it's something
we did our greatest
proximity to something
bigger than ourselves
how my grandfather
would sit waiting and
see the local newscaster
getting her hair
done the quality
of the fountains and block glass
midways shifting brighter
and more glittering
the decades of my youth
in the American '90s
though I don't know
what it's like anymore
not all malls
are the same and
this was ours
where we went
for hamburgers
the juice-colored juke box
with my grandmother where
my aunt then brother
worked through a series
of stores decades and
uniforms chocolates
gadgets and soaps
I forgot how
much time I
spent at the mall
and money moments

of recognition
or its opposite
my first starburst
age two or so
the chlorine
of cold coins wet
from the fountain
the vinyl pile
of princesses
in the toy store
the warm pull
of cookies the only
snack we ever bought
away from home
the glycerin and hot
sun of soap the party
bass of Abercrombie
like we had a friend
with a vacation house
in the pine forests
of somewhere desirable
because someone chose
us to be presented
with these t-shirts
sweaters and low-
rise jeans how
one field trip
we went straight
from the museum
for Gauguin to
the mall for lunch
and there we all were
that day and never again
having arrived
in the bright perfumed
public of the suburbs

DEBT RITUAL: VALUE

if money is valor
if I am worthy
like a strong weight
a balance a measure
if I lean on the scale
if something helps me
if a heavy ghost waits
for the balance
for tipping towards it
how large I am
how large the ghost
I trace its outline
on the dirt with a stick
trace my debt
next to it say
I choose
an outline to lie
in lie in it
until I die
or become larger
they will honor
me my touch
my contactless body
they will seek
to make me public
or refuse this
of me they will
ask me to buy
a piece of ground
from under some
one's body
they will trace
my ghosts wherever

I go without
they say I need to
be participating
in the solution
they say they have
the solution
for me to
participate in

DEBT RITUAL: MASS

gather continuously a mass
of objects in proportion to
interest capitalized on your
balance all the better
if you must use money to
acquire these objects as this
institutes a feedback loop
which will help your mass
and balance grow ever more
quickly as you acquire with
ever greater haste material
as weight to ballast your
balance
as you
you
say I
I
am worthy
I am
worthy I
am
worthy un-
til the balance balances or
until you have nothing left

DEBT RITUAL: CLASS

*(with a debt owed, formally, to
Tyehimba Jess's* Olio)

debt means	my household things
even the rich	are possible
can feel poor	with my work
a balance	nothing else
accumulation	when my job's gone
hours in	the rain outside

the apartment
daylight passing
and fading into

the couch	someone else's
things picked	stocks
to signify	making money
just so	I see
there are	in-
differences	-what is
though	not for me

DEBT RITUAL: NANTUCKET

There was something I didn't know about money until
     college
until Nantucket pants in pastel chino with whale appliques
worn seriously walking past the dining hall to go out
     Friday night
but that isn't money that's pants that's signification
okay of Nantucket where I still have never been
but I guess that's also a romanticized rusticity
as in weathered boards and mismatched wooden furniture
I read the English upper classes only
use bar soap in cracked and ancient cakes
like that there's nothing more expensive than that
what perches at the absolute fathomless ceaseless
     continuation
of the ocean unadulterated except by refinement
to the bare possibility of habitation even the linens
are old and linen or so I imagine the type
of money that's evident so that money is
an aesthetic a quiet language of material
which of course is not money but signification
money's something else

DEBT RITUAL: CONGEAL

(with debt owed to Karl Marx's Capital)

I turn my head and make it holy
I turn my breath and it congeals
I mark the carcass with the knowing cuts
I read these on the internet and see
into the body the musculature
the skin runs gelatinous along the countertop
it's Tuesday I am making dinner
the body has its own temporalities
hunger and exhaustion not separate
from work the distant bodies
keeping the body of my dinner
alive killing it and putting it
in plastic keeping it cold
moving it around taking
my money for it I pay
a late fee at the gym
my credit card number changed
for another when someone
on the internet takes it
buys something with my
money until the company
cancels it my body
running unaccustomed
to such work but built
for it for labor
cooking dinner an email
comes with the DNA test
my father bought me
for Christmas the story
we already knew poor
and Irish my father

age nine comes home
alone cooks a chicken
while his mother works
in the bank his father
drinks the specificity
of the map though
the small circles
the parishes and abbeys
one day's walk five thousand
extant speakers
language before English
mostly gone now
bodies of cousins
the suburbs of Chicago
Boston New York
factory jobs Sunday Mass
it matters who I make
mine matters the bodies
I call the city those that
do the work matters
my family made money
when Irish got called white
I'm the first five generations
into America not born
in a mill city of someone
not from Munster and someone
maps my body my family
definitively with science
for the future the internet
and church and time
has past body matter
and mass I turn my head
I turn my breath

DEBT RITUAL: DRIFT

(owing a debt to Roland Barthes
The Pleasure of the Text *and*
Lisa Robertson *"Time in the Codex")*

an idea passes over the city
the lake wanting to be with us
the cloud shade of desire
the void blush accumulating
on time and its architecture
like other ideas I memorize
or which make themselves in me
and in which I choose of necessity
to live an idea makes good
neighbors a good storm a good
way out for someone I am way
in with someone hearing
their teeth and breathing
hearing the orthographic noises
of their thinking I am way in
with the city the way it isn't going
I am not going with it
something layered on
the surface something stupid
and intractable about me
a text a building someone else
some other time was here
of this same hasty ritual
and its drift what gives
and what is given back

DEBT RITUAL: MATERIAL

the wild interior
the motion imperceptible of dill fronds reaching
      toward the pane of window light
the pale green of difficulty
the dust arrives each week on the carpet
the hair falls from the head (our heads)
the crumb from the loaf (our breakfasts)
the air marked with particles a wind blows through
the compost grows warm the heat of eggshells and
      squash
a rock achieves and refuses stasis
it takes heat to animate thought
reciprocal bodily proximity
one week the bruised brain makes us materialists
the hazy too-brightness of all sound and image
the window and the television
all manner of symbol alike

DEBT RITUAL: MIDDLE

I want what is the difference
between occupier and occupant
a receptivity in time and space
the almost passive almost object
what what is subtracted between
a dense rye loaf I baked today
and the thirty-four years I ate
bread I had not made
the space made by the existence
of a general loaf of soft white
bread in a soft plastic single sleeve
from the shelves of a 7-Eleven or Pathmark
and the occurrence of the soft interior
of this as toast margarine and sweet
milky tea on a vinyl tablecloth
with yesterday's crumbs and cactuses
haphazardly potted in the window
the exterior stairs go by passing
between this heritage and another
I cribbed second-hand a difference
between occupying and occupation
a difference in intention a difference
between the apple shower gel bought
at the mall aged twelve or thirteen
and the herbs that scent Marseilles soap
since the twelfth or thirteenth century
the difference between someone
talking on tv and me and my friend
making videos in the backyard
in our summer clothes it's close
isn't it all this difference for some
of us somewhere in the middle

sometimes I want only the flat grey
blue middle of the lake on a cloudy day
the reeds in the winter when it will snow
sometimes to flatten sometimes to rise

DEBT RITUAL: MUSKRAT LODGE

this is a small poem
for the muskrat lodge
made of reed
and the fox tracks
frozen into the slush-ice
for the way
being outside
these months
shows
the temporary
natures of structures
of course
the interior
is only a
spatial metaphor
for temporal
engagement
everyone
was everywhere
all along
making with
what was
close at hand

DEBT RITUAL: SAVINGS BANK

the building on the corner of 96th and Amsterdam
a temple in the Greek idiom
pillars set down directly
on the sidewalk
with presidents (Jefferson):
Save and teach all you are
interested
to save: thus pave
the way for moral and material
success (Lincoln):
Teach economy. That is
one of the first and highest
virtues. It begins with saving
money. The 1920s took
down two tenements to
put it there. Now it's
a CVS and a private
preschool. I could say
some obvious things
about tenements preschool
tuition and who might save
what. I could say something
about the instructional
ambitions of bank walls
American presidents
and the Grecian ideals
of political and economic
American architecture
like was this place doomed
to be an expensive preschool
by the tone of the inscriptions
over its doors.
I guess the advice is
basically sound to keep

carefully what you don't
need today and let
it grow. I could add
the bank was the first
to welcome women,
immigrants, that it served
wealth then maybe
against wealth that it was
done in by high interest
rates by bad investments
by the 1970s I could say
something obvious
about what the wall doesn't know
about 21st century interest rates
or about need and excess
about precarity or that
my life-long poverty-line
grandmother's advice was
if you have it use it
for what you were
interested in
and instantly feel
I need to defend her
nevertheless near-
complete and necessary
frugality the insistence
on virtue not accidental
the poem's already there
in the words on the corner
in the lobby now full
of light medical equipment
and snack food
a place we might have
walked to bought
some small un-
necessary thing

DEBT RITUAL: BUS

one kind of public life
is on a bus
to work the counter
at the bank
your kids letting
themselves in
home after
school making
dinner a life
of not driving
was gendered
or classed
the bus was
available
that's what
city
means history
of public
transportation
worn into
pavement
lines of heat
driving through
that place

DEBT RITUAL: UTOPIA

an orientation toward evening
okay the sun is going down first
golden purples of snow the late
stage for being this end of storm
says one way to be is you two
and a baby and an apartment
and in the afternoon you go out
all together I mean I guess
it's possible to move through time
and space together and money's
adjacency to this
incidental but not transcendent
so a child does not know
at some point what it is
so the body's organic
life as well walking without
money the sky does glow
blue and deep and bright
where clouds part after sunset
going back inside money
does buy this place
of rest and warmth

ACKNOWLEDGMENTS

2024. "debt ritual: bus," "debt ritual: value," "debt ritual: mass," "debt ritual: snack," *Still Point.* (Forthcoming, print and online)

2023. "Debt Ritual: Mall." *Yalobusha Review.* (Online)

2022. "Debt Ritual: Congeal," "Debt Ritual: Nantucket." *Bennington Review.* (Print)

2022. "Debt Ritual: Utopia." *Dusie Blog.* (Online.)

2021. "Debt Ritual: Class," *Tupelo Quarterly.* (Online)

2021. "debt ritual: savings bank," "debt ritual: originary objects,""debt ritual: drift." *Tagvverk.* (Online)

2021. "debt ritual: middle," *P-Queue.* (Print).

2021. "debt ritual: oysters." *Third Coast.* (Print).

2021. "Threshold," "Debt Ritual: Muskrat Lodge," "Debt Ritual: Material." *Annulet.* (Online)

2019. "debt ritual (grain)." *Poets.org University Poetry Prizes.* (Online)

FONO
GRAꟻ

1. **Eileen Myles**—*Aloha/irish trees* (LP)

2. **Rae Armantrout**—*Conflation* (LP)

3. **Alice Notley**—*Live in Seattle* (LP)

4. **Harmony Holiday**—*The Black Saint and the Sinnerman* (LP)

5. **Susan Howe & Nathaniel Mackey**—*STRAY: A Graphic Tone* (LP)

6. **Annelyse Gelman & Jason Grier**—*About Repulsion* (EP)

7. **Joshua Beckman**—*Some Mechanical Poems To Be Read Aloud* (print)

8. **Dao Strom**—*Instrument/ Traveler's Ode* (print; cassette tape)

9. **Douglas Kearney & Val Jeanty**—*Fodder* (LP)

10. **Mark Leidner**—*Returning the Sword to the Stone* (print)

11. **Charles Valle**—*Proof of Stake: An Elegy* (print)

12. **Emily Kendal Frey**—*LOVABILITY* (print)

13. **Brian Laidlaw and the Family Trade**—*THIS ASTER: adaptations of Emile Nelligan* (LP)

14. **Nathaniel Mackey and The Creaking Breeze Ensemble**—*Fugitive Equation* (compact disc)

15. *FE Magazine* (print)

16. **Brandi Katherine Herrera**—*MOTHER IS A BODY* (print)

17. **Jan Verberkmoes**—*Firewatch* (print)

18. **Krystal Languell**—*Systems Thinking with Flowers* (print)

19. **Matvei Yankelevich**—*Dead Winter* (print)

20. **Cody-Rose Clevidence**—*Dearth & God's Green Mirth* (print)

21. **Hilary Plum**—*Hole Studies* (print)

22. **John Ashbery**—*Live at Sanders Theatre, 1976* (LP)

23. **Alice Notley**—*The Speak Angel Series* (print)

24. **Alice Notley**—*Early Works* (print)

25. **Joshua Marie Wilkinson**—*Trouble Finds You* (print)

26. **Timmy Straw**—*The Thomas Salto* (print)

27. **Audre Lorde**—*At Fassett Studio, 1970* (LP)

28. **Gabriel Palacios**—*A Ten Peso Burial For Which Truth I Sign* (print)

29. **Isabel Zapata, trans. Robin Myers**—*A Whale Is a Country* (print)

30. **Callum Angus**—*Cataract* (print)

31. **Eds. Dao Strom & Jyothi Natarajan**—*FE/De-Canon Anthology* (print)

32. **Cody-Rose Clevidence**—*The Grimace of Eden, Now* (print)

33. **Jaydra Johnson**—*Low: Notes on Art and Trash* (print)

34. **Jaime Gil de Biedma**—*If Only For a Moment (I'll Never Be Young Again)* (print)

Fonograf Editions is a registered 501(c)(3) nonprofit organization. Find more information about the press at: fonografeditions.com.

BUNNY

1. **Warren Longmire**—*BIRD/DIZ [an erased history of bebop]* (print)

2. **Bill Carty**—*We Sailed on the Lake* (print)

3. **Zoe Tuck**—*Bedroom Vowel* (print)

4. **Michael Wheaton**—*Home Movies* (print)

5. **Jennifer Quartararo**—*An Aribtrary Formation of Unspecified Value* (print)

6. **Matt Broaddus**—*Deeper the Tropics* (print)

7. **Katie Naughton**—*Debt Ritual* (print)

Inspired by the work of the multitudinous artist Ray Johnson, BUNNY is an imprint of Fonograf Editions. Publishing a wide variety of works, BUNNY is looking towards the future while thinking about the past.